ROYAL SCHOOL
OF NEEDLEWORK

D0409189

Essential Stitch Guide

CANVASWORK

:h Guide

CANVASWORK

RACHEL DOYLE

SEARCH PRESS

First published in Great Britain 2013
Search Press Limited
Wellwood, North Farm Road,
Tunbridge Wells, Kent TN2 3DR
Copyright © Rachel Doyle 2013
Photographs by Paul Bricknell at Search Press studios
Photographs and design copyright © Search Press Ltd. 2013
Photography of Hampton Court Palace with kind permission
from Historic Royal Palaces.

ISBN: 978-1-84448-587-1

Readers are permitted to reproduce any of the patterns in
this book for their personal use, or for purposes of selling for
charity, free of charge and without the prior permission of the
Publishers. Any use of the patterns for commercial purposes is
not permitted without the prior permission of the Publishers.

Suppliers
If you have any difficulty obtaining any of the materials
and equipment mentioned in this book, please visit the
Search Press website: www.searchpress.com

For more details about the work of the Royal School of
Needlework, including courses, tours, our Studio, tutors and
where some of our work can be seen, please go to our website:
www.royal-needlework.org.uk

Page 1
Figs
*A canvas shaded piece worked
in tent stitch (see page 86) with
a cashmere stitch (see page 43)
background. Worked in crewel
wool. 21st Century. (Author's
personal collection)*

Page 2
Mabel
*A miniature canvas piece. 21st
Century. (Personal collection of
Sophie Long)*

Page 3
Italian Bargello work
*A sample piece of Florentine
or Bargello work (see page 54)
combining silk and wool.
Italian, 17th/18th century.
(RSN Collection)*

Opposite
Stitch sampler
*Incomplete, worked on fine
canvas. Late 19th or early 20th
century. (RSN Collection)*

Printed in China

CONTENTS

THE ROYAL SCHOOL OF NEEDLEWORK

The Royal School of Needlework was founded in 1872 by Lady Victoria Welby because she wanted to ensure the arts and techniques of high quality hand embroidery were kept alive. At the time, Berlin wool work, a form of canvaswork, was all the rage, almost to the exclusion of all other techniques. The RSN began to train people in the wide range of historic techniques from blackwork to silk shading and from metal thread work to whitework. Working with designers such as William Morris, Walter Crane and Edward Burne-Jones, they created pieces for exhibitions in the US and Paris, and for private commissions.

Since then, the RSN has used these techniques to make new works for a wide variety of organisations from cathedrals and synagogues to historic buildings and commercial organisations as well as for individuals. We have also worked for every British monarch since Queen Victoria.

Today, the RSN is at the forefront of teaching hand embroidery techniques to the highest standard and welcomes people from all over the world on to its courses every year. We also have an extensive collection of embroidered textiles and archival material which acts as a fantastic resource for ideas and inspiration. Visitors to our rooms at Hampton Court Palace, whether for classes or tours, can see a changing range of works from the Collection on display.

While setting a high standard, the RSN exists to encourage more people to participate in hand embroidery and to this end, runs courses from beginner level in every technique, for those who want to pursue embroidery as a leisure interest, right through to our professional Certificate, Diploma and Foundation Degree for those who want to develop their future careers in embroidered textiles. While we are trying to increase the number of locations where courses are held, we are well aware that Hampton Court Palace, a few other UK centres and San Francisco and Tokyo are not easily accessible to many people who would like to explore embroidery through the RSN approach, hence this series of Essential Stitch Guides.

Each book is written by an RSN Graduate Apprentice who has spent three years at the RSN learning techniques and then applying them in the RSN Studio, working on pieces from our Collection or on customers' contemporary and historic pieces. All are also tutors on our courses.

Alongside the actual stitches and historic examples of the technique you will also find a selection of works by the author and other RSN Apprentices and Students to show how a technique can really be used in new ways. While the RSN uses traditional stitch techniques as its medium, we believe that they can be used to create very contemporary works to ensure hand embroidery is not just kept alive, but flourishes into the future. We hope these images will inspire you to explore and develop your own work.

Opposite and below

Hampton Court Palace, Surrey, home of the Royal School of Needlework.

INTRODUCTION

Before I joined the Royal School of Needlework the only canvaswork pieces I had done were charted designs, followed closely and exactly, and always in tent stitch. During my three year apprenticeship at the school I was introduced to canvas stitches and the possibilities of producing my own designs.

Canvaswork is often overlooked as a creative embroidery technique. Try not to see the formal grid of the canvas as a restriction. Instead, look at it as you would any other background fabric – a space to fill with your embroidery. Similarly, do not assume that your canvaswork has to be worked in wool. Anything that will fit in the eye of a needle and through the holes of the canvas can be used – ribbon, silk, stranded cotton, metallic threads – and, of course, you can also apply embellishment to a piece such as beads and sequins.

It is surprising how much detail you can put into a canvas piece, so almost any design can be adapted to this technique, be it a delicate landscape or a bold abstract design. There will always be a stitch to suit any surface or shape.

There are too many canvas stitches out there to illustrate in just one book, so I have chosen a broad cross-section of useful stitches to get you started. Hopefully these will be a starting point for your canvaswork and you will develop and add to what is illustrated here.

A good starting point is to sample some stitches. Explore the book and start with the ones to which you are drawn. They may inspire a design themselves. My piece *Swedish Boat Houses* (see page 29) was inspired by a sample of Fern stitch. The strong vertical pattern married up perfectly to the texture of the houses.

The stitch sampler on the facing page was worked during the process of writing this book. It is a great reference piece for me to see the texture and scale of each stitch and I can now use this to design future projects.

The following pages will discuss the process of working a canvas piece, from choosing your canvas and picking a design to how to begin stitching it. There is then a stitch library from which to pick your stitches and throughout the book there are many canvas designs to provide you with inspiration.

I hope this book will give its readers the confidence to pick up a needle and realise the potential of this expressive technique.

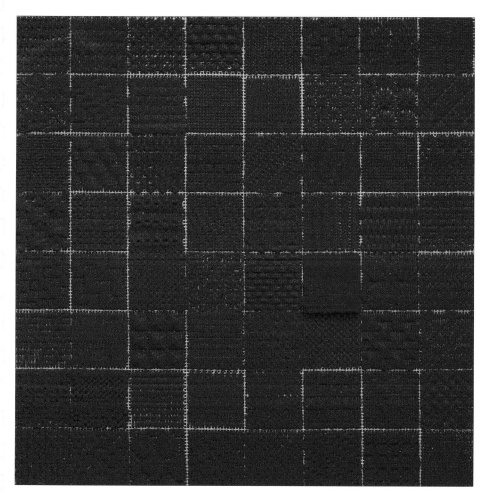

Canvaswork stitch sampler

A sampler of sixty-four one-inch squares stitched by the author. All are worked in the same colour crewel wool, but each is a different stitch. This piece shows the wide variety of texture that can be achieved with canvas stitches. 21st century. (Author's personal collection)

THE HISTORY OF CANVASWORK

Canvaswork is an embroidery technique using counted stitches on an openly woven base fabric. In America the technique is called needlepoint. It is often incorrectly called tapestry work, which is actually a woven technique. Canvaswork was sometimes used to replicate tapestry and this may be the origin of the confusion of names.

It is difficult to say when the first canvas pieces were worked. It was used in a basic form on mediaeval vestments and furnishings, but it is really during the second half of the 16th century that canvaswork in its current form became a part of everyday life.

All manner of domestic furnishings were covered in canvaswork, from wall hangings, and screens to the unusual 'table carpets' that were popular at the time. This work was more often than not stitched by amateur embroiderers at home, although some professional workshops did exist. The designs were often pictorial, heraldic, floral or simply geometric.

An important collection of canvaswork from this time was produced at Hardwick Hall in Derbyshire. Bess of Hardwick, the lady of the house, produced many embroideries together with Mary Queen of Scots, who was under house arrest at the hall. The embroideries are on permanent display at Hardwick Hall. The Oxburgh Hangings (c. 1570) are a series of canvaswork panels that were cut out and applied to a velvet background. Small canvas 'slips' applied to another fabric was a technique that was widely used at the time to keep the drape of the fabric.

The Hatton Garden Hangings, now housed at the Victoria and Albert Museum in London, are another important example of canvaswork. These six large panels were originally mounted as stretched wall coverings and used to decorate a room as a cheaper alternative to tapestries. They date from around 1690, and were rediscovered in 1896 behind many layers of paper and paint in a house in Hatton Gardens. Professionally worked, they show classical columns surrounded by foliage, birds and animals. They include a variety of stitches including Hungarian (see page 63), rice (see page 82), eyelet (see page 37) and tent (see page 86).

As interior fashions changed so did the canvaswork. Table carpets became floor coverings and cushions became upholstered chairs and sofas. Many smaller canvas items such as book covers, shoes, pincushions and purses were also produced. However, by the end of the eighteenth century, there was a serious decline in canvaswork.

During the nineteenth century, canvaswork became once again a huge domestic pastime. At the start of the 1800s, charts for canvaswork designs started being produced in Berlin. The charts were handpainted on graph paper, with one square representing one intersection of canvas. Although expensive, these were an instant success. Wool from Saxony, spun in Gotha and dyed in Berlin was sold with these kits, giving them their name of Berlin wool work. These beautiful wools were available in a well blended colour range alongside canvas made of silk spun around cotton.

Mr Wilks of Regent Street, London, a leading needlework supplier, began importing the patterns and wools in the 1830s and soon the popularity of Berlin wool work spread through the UK and then the rest of the world.

By the middle of the century the patterns and even the wools were being produced in many countries, although the name was kept.

Painted canvas design

A hand-painted Berlin wool work chart for a pear border design. 19th century. (RSN Collection)

Industrialisation brought mass production of patterns and soon some 14,000 were readily and cheaply available. The delicate individual designs of the original Berlin wool work were soon lost to endless repeats of the same designs, stitched with harsh synthetically dyed wool from the 1850s onwards. The stitches used were always a tent or cross stitch. The only developments to the style were the introduction of beads and also plush work, which gave a sculptural effect.

The decline of Berlin wool work began in the 1870s. Designers such as William Morris turned away from the restrictions of canvas grids to more freeing surface embroidery techniques, such as crewelwork.

Canvas kits never quite went away and mass-produced designs were still available. In the 1920s the Royal School of Needlework began hand painting canvases, often based on historical designs. These canvases were usually for interiors such as cushions, screens and chair seats and would be worked by individuals at home.

Modern canvas kits are available in the form of a printed design with wools supplied. The unique interpretation of a design by the embroiderer is lost, and the huge variety of stitches available is reduced to simple tent stitch. However, there is a small but growing interest in reviving the individuality of pieces of work. Skilled embroiderers are creating new designs using a much wider variety of stitches to create contemporary pieces of art.

Figurative roundel with floral border

A canvas piece more reminiscent of a stumpwork design. The same designs were often used for different techniques. Canvaswork on linen worked in silk and wool. 18th century. (RSN Collection)

Materials

FRAMES

To keep an even tension on your work, you should always work a canvas piece in a frame. The type of frame you use will depend on the size of the piece you are working. A frame with a stand or clamp is generally the easiest to use as you will not have to hold the frame with one hand, while stitching with the other.

Slate frame

A slate frame is a large, strong, wooden frame which will give you the tightest possible tension on your canvas. They are made up of four bars: two have webbing attached and two have holes for split pins. A slate frame rests horizontally on a pair of wooden trestles, allowing the embroiderer to keep both hands free for stitching. This will speed up your stitching significantly, but does limit the portability of your work while it is being stitched. Slate frames with a stand attached are also available. Slate frames are available in a variety of sizes, but I find that the most comfortable size to use is a 61cm (24in) frame.

Ring frame

A ring frame is made up of two hoops between which you sandwich your canvas. These are great for smaller projects, but you must keep tightening the frame as it will slacken off quickly. Ring frames are available in a wide variety of sizes.

Deep ring frames are more suited to canvaswork as narrow embroidery hoops do not grip the canvas as well. Ring frames with a dowel attached can be used with either a seat stand or a barrel clamp, which attaches to a table. These frames leave both hands free to stitch.

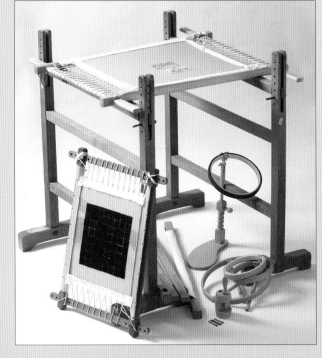

Anticlockwise from top: A framed-up 61cm (24in) slate frame resting on a pair of trestles. A smaller slate frame with a worked canvas piece framed up on it. An unframed slate frame and split pins. Various sized ring frames, a seat stand and a table barrel clamp.

CANVAS

The canvas is the foundation of your work and its structure, colour and scale should all be considered before starting.

Single canvas

Canvas is a strong, even, openly woven fabric with clearly visible holes in it. Single or mono canvas is suitable for most projects and is woven with the same number of threads per inch in both warp and weft.

Double canvas

Double canvas is woven with pairs of threads in the warp and weft. These pairs of threads can be stitched over as one thread, or individually as two threads, giving you two scales of canvas in one fabric.

A selection of white and antique canvas pieces. Always store your canvas rolled to prevent creases.

Colours

The majority of commercially available canvas kits are worked on white canvas, but for most projects I would recommend using a brown canvas called antique. The more neutral colour of antique canvas is far easier to cover with stitches than a bright white canvas. If you were working a project with a lot of light colours in it then the opposite would be true and a white canvas would be more forgiving to use.

Scale

The threads per inch (tpi) of a canvas is important to consider. The higher the number, the finer the canvas. The finer the canvas, the more detail you will be able to put into your work. Conversely, the lower the tpi the quicker your piece will be to work. Students at the Royal School of Needlework generally work on 18 tpi canvas for small designs. This is quite a fine canvas and allows a lot of detail to be put into the work.

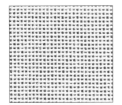
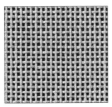
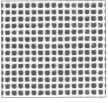
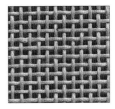

White 24 tpi canvas – a very fine canvas.

Antique 18 tpi canvas – a fairly fine canvas.

White 14 tpi canvas – a medium scale canvas.

Antique 10 tpi canvas – an open canvas, unsuitable for very intricate designs.

THREADS

Within reason almost any thread can work on a canvas piece. The only restriction is fitting it through the eye of a needle and through the holes of the canvas. Usually several strands of thread will be used in the needle at once. These strands can all be of the same thread or different threads can be used at once. A single strand of metallic thread for instance might be combined with several crewel wool strands to give a subtle shimmer to an area. It is always a good idea to sample the threads you have chosen to see how many strands are needed to cover the canvas. Too few and you will have gaps, too many and the canvas can be distorted.

Stranded cotton

Stranded cotton is a strong hardwearing thread. It is a great thread to use for canvaswork as it comes in a variety of colours and shades.

Stranded cotton is smooth and it will have a slight sheen to it when worked correctly. Always separate the strands of the cotton and ply them back together for the flattest possible finish.

Silk and metallic threads

Fancy decorative threads will add interest to your canvaswork. Silk will give a great shine to your piece but it is a more delicate thread to use and it is not as strong as a stranded cotton.

Metallic threads are often very fine so it is a good idea to use them in the needle with another thread.

Wool

Wool is a staple of canvaswork and like stranded cotton, it is also available in a wide variety of colours and shades.

Crewel wool is very fine so you will need to use several strands at once, while tapestry wool is fairly thick and can often be used with just a single thread. Wool is hardwearing and will have a smooth, matt texture to it when stitched.

NEEDLES

Canvaswork is a counted technique and stitch placement is (for the most part) restricted by the holes of the canvas. Your needle should go through these holes and not pierce the fabric, so it is always best to use a blunt tapestry needle rather than a sharp embroidery needle. It is much easier to guide a blunt needle through the canvas than a sharp one, and you are also less likely to catch the thread of any previous stitches.

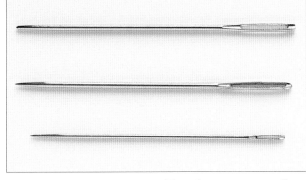

Top to bottom: tapestry needle, chenille needle, embroidery needle.

A sharp chenille needle should only be used when you want to pierce the threads of the canvas. This would only be for overstitched details once the majority of a piece is stitched.

The sizes of both tapestry and chenille needles are the same, and the smaller the number, the larger the needle. The larger the needle, the easier it is to work with. There are no rules as to the size of needle you use compared with the tpi of your canvas (see page 13), but the threaded needle does need to pass through the holes smoothly. If you are forcing it through then it is too large and can widen the holes of the canvas. The easiest way to check is to thread the needle with the appropriate number of strands and make sure that it passes smoothly through the canvas holes.

Tapestry needles

Tapestry needles have a blunt end and a long eye to ease threading. The eye is the widest part of the needle, so make sure that the complete needle passes through your canvas easily.

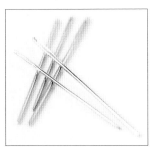

Chenille needles

Chenille needles look the same as a tapestry needle but with a sharp end. Again, compared with an embroidery needle they have a much longer eye for threading several strands through.

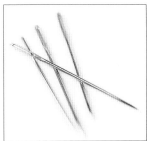

OTHER MATERIALS

In addition to your canvas, frame, needles and thread it will also be useful to have the following equipment.

String, bracing needle, tape measure, buttonhole thread, pins and **pincushion** These are used when framing up a slate frame.

Webbing This is cotton tape that is used when framing up a slate frame.

Fabric scissors These are used for cutting soft fabrics, particularly the webbing tape.

General purpose scissors Canvas is quite a tough material, so do not use your best fabric scissors. Instead, use a large pair of paper scissors.

Embroidery scissors and **angled embroidery scissors** For the stitching you will need a sharp pair of embroidery scissors. Straight and bent scissors are both useful for cutting threads close to the canvas surface.

Thimble I always stitch with a thimble, but not everyone finds them useful.

Needle case This is useful for storing your needles safely in between projects.

Waterproof fineliner pens, pencil, paper, tracing paper and **ruler** These are used for creating and developing your design.

Screwdriver A screwdriver will help you tighten your ring frame.

Tweezers I like to have a pair of pointed and flat-ended tweezers in my sewing box. Both are helpful if you do have to unpick any stitches. Use them from both the front and back of the work to get every fibre out.

Mellor A mellor can be useful for laying down threads smoothly.

Waterproof marker pens and **machine thread** These materials are used when transferring your design.

Ring nose pliers A small pair of pliers is great for pulling stubborn needles through when weaving in on the back.

Shade card This is a useful tool to help when ordering materials for your project. Simply hold it next to your source photograph and pick the colour that matches best.

Dutch Flower

This design is worked on a very fine 24tpi canvas, making the stitching appear to be painted. 20th Century. (RSN Collection)

Rice stitch pencil case

A canvas pencil case decorated using rice stitch blended from one shade to the next in horizontal lines. 21st century. (Author's personal collection)

FRAMING UP

Canvas work is a densely stitched technique so it is very important to have a firm tension on the canvas when it is worked. Due to the diagonal nature of a lot of the stitches, the canvas tends to distort into a diamond shape if it is not tensioned properly. For these reasons, working a canvas piece in the hand should be avoided if possible, and you should work on a frame.

There are two main methods of framing a piece of canvas. For small designs a ring frame can be used. For any designs that will not fit comfortably into a ring frame, a slate frame should be used.

PREPARING A SLATE FRAME

A very tight tension can be achieved on this type of frame, but it will slacken off with use. Always retighten the string of a slate frame each time you sit down to work.

Slate frames are available in a variety of sizes, but I find that the most comfortable size to use is a 61cm (24in) frame, as used in this example. A 50 x 50cm (19¾ x 19¾in) piece of canvas fits well on to a frame of this size.

1 Cut a 50 x 50cm (19¾ x 19¾in) square of the correct tpi canvas that you wish to use, making sure to cut along the grain so it will sit straight. Cut off any selvedge to ensure that the tension is equal throughout the square.

2 Fold 1cm (½in) of the canvas back on itself along the grain, then repeat on the other side (see inset).

3 On the frame arm, find the centre of the webbing and make a mark with a pencil. Measure from the inner edge of the holes in the arm, not the end of the webbing. This is because the webbing is not always in the centre of the arm.

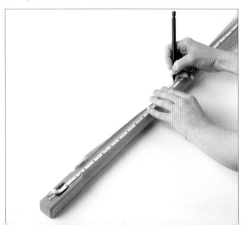

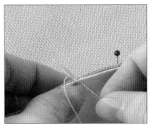

4 Fold the canvas in half across the turned-back edge as shown to find the centre (see inset), then unfold it. Align the centre of the canvas with the centre of the webbing on the arm and secure it with a pin.

5 Working from the centre outwards, pin the fabric to the webbing, spacing the pins approximately 2.5cm (1in) apart.

6 Thread a chenille needle with buttonhole thread and tie a knot in the end. Starting from the centre of the canvas, oversew 2–3mm down from the edge to secure the thread.

Tip

The turned-back edge should be back to back with the underside of the webbing.

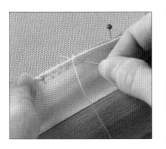

7 Work long and short stitch to the right, keeping the stitches about 2–3mm apart and removing the pins as you work.

8 Once you reach the edge, finish your thread with a couple of oversew stitches. Start again in the centre with a new thread and work to the other edge.

9 Repeat stages 3–8 on the other end of the canvas.

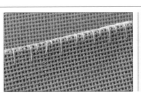

Tip

Securing the canvas with long and short stitches ensures that the tension is spread over different rows of the canvas, holding it more securely in place.

10 Cut a piece of webbing to fit the side of the canvas. Place it three-quarters on the canvas, with the rest overhanging.

11 Pin the webbing in place, then knot and thread a chenille needle with buttonhole thread. Work basting stitch along the webbing (diagonally on the front, straight on the back), removing pins as you go.

12 Finish with a couple of oversewn straight stitches, then secure a strip of webbing to the other side in the same way.

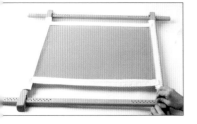

13 Insert the arms in the frame and put split pins in the same holes on either side so that the fabric is tight.

Tip

Ensure that the holes in the arms are a mirror image of each other when you insert them, as this helps to ensure that the tension is even.

14 Place the frame on the trestles and thread a bracing needle on to a ball of string. Sew into the webbing around the arm, making large stitches approximately 2.5cm (1in) apart. Try not to go through the canvas.

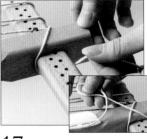

15 Repeat on the other arm. Rest the frame on the floor and increase the tension by resting your foot on the end of the roller arm.

16 Move the holding peg to the next hole to secure the tension. Repeat on the other side to get the canvas taut. Only tighten by working one hole at a time.

17 Rest the frame back on the trestles and pick up the loose end of the string at one of the corners. Loop it round and under the arm, then make a loop with a twist (see inset).

18 Pass the loop under the first part of the string that is holding the tension.

19 Make a second loop and pass it through the first, over the string.

20 Pull the second loop towards the canvas to close the first loop and secure the knot.

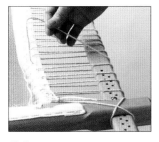 

21 Working away from the knot, gradually tighten the canvas by pulling the string tight against the arm.

22 Tie a slipknot on the other end to secure the string and complete the tensioning on this side.

23 Repeat on the other side to finish framing up.

PREPARING A RING FRAME

A ring frame is a much more portable way of working a small canvas piece. Deep ring frames, as used in this example, are more suited to canvas as narrow embroidery hoops do not grip the canvas as well.

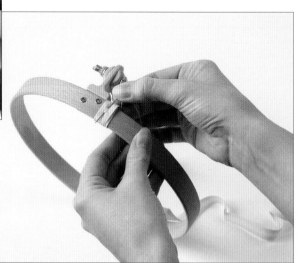

1 Starting at the top of the inner frame, wrap bias binding around the frame two or three times (see inset), then use sewing thread and an embroidery needle to secure it with a holding stitch.

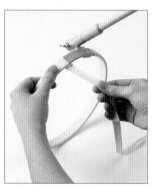

2 Working clockwise, start to wrap the binding around the frame. Open up the leading edge of the bias binding as you work, and overlap half of the previous bit of binding with each wrap.

3 Continue wrapping the bias binding around the frame all the way round.

4 When you reach the end, fold the leading edge of the bias binding back in and wrap it round the frame two or three times.

5 Holding the binding tight, cut the excess away, then fold the end back under itself and oversew the end on the inside of the inner ring.

6 Wrap the outer ring in the same way, making the stitches on the outside of the ring. This will prevent the stitches rubbing once the fabric is sandwiched between the two prepared rings.

7 Cut a piece of canvas slightly larger than the outer ring and place it on top of the outer ring. Place the inner ring on the top of the canvas and push it down in the middle.

8 Tighten the frame with a screwdriver to finish preparing the ring frame.

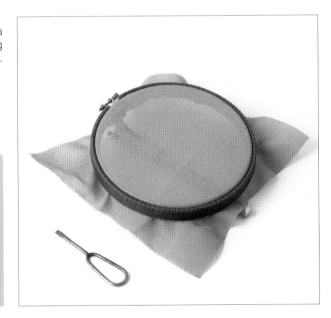

Note

Do not be tempted to work a large design in a small ring frame and to move the ring frame around the design. This will not keep an even tension across the whole piece and may damage areas of worked design that are crushed between the two rings of the ring frame.

DESIGN

The majority of canvaswork done today is worked from a chart or on to a painted canvas, and designing your own canvas piece can seem like a daunting task. However, by sourcing your own design and choosing your own stitches you will create a much more expressive and individual piece. By working only from a drawn outline your stitching will be totally unique to you.

FINDING INSPIRATION

The inspiration for a canvas design can come from anywhere. Using a photograph is the simplest method, or working from one of your own paintings or drawings. A good image to work from will have plenty of areas large enough to fit a few repeats of a canvas stitch pattern. A design with lots of different textures in it will allow you to experiment with different stitches.

USING YOUR IMAGE

Once you have chosen your design, you will need to work out the best size to use it. Print out a few copies at different sizes if you have a digital version of the design; and use a photocopier to make larger and smaller copies of the design if you do not.

Place these side by side in size order and eliminate any that are too big (where the effect of the stitches will be lost) and too small (where the stitch patterns will be awkward to fit). When you have decided on the size you will work your design, make sure you also have a clear copy of your image at a size that is easy to see all the detail.

The original photograph, and a slightly enlarged version (see inset), made by scanning the photograph on to a computer then printing it out at a larger scale.

CREATING A LINE DRAWING

To turn your image into a simple line drawing, you will now need to trace the design. Use a sharp pencil and a ruler for the outside edges and any straight lines in the design. Take care to make this tracing as accurate as possible.

1 Use a fine permanent marker to trace the main outlines. Try to aim for large block areas and do not get over-detailed.

2 Photocopy the tracing on to plain paper.

3 Use a permanent marker to go over the lines of the photocopy to make a final drawing.

TRANSFERRING YOUR DESIGN TO CANVAS

At this stage, the edge of the design is tacked on to the canvas and the design is drawn within this. The tacking stitches will be removed once the design is complete. Be careful not to go over the edges as you do not want pen marks to show outside your stitched design.

1 Use a ruler to measure the outline of your design.

2 Thread a tapestry needle with a contrasting machine thread and tack an outline on to the canvas at the same size.

3 Hold the final drawing behind the canvas and trace the main shapes only on to the canvas with a thick waterproof permanent marker. Do not trace the outline.

PICKING COLOURS FOR YOUR DESIGN

Once the linework is complete (see page 25), you will need to pick appropriate coloured yarns for the design. One of the benefits of using stranded cotton and crewel wools for shaded designs is the range of colours available. Colour ranges are usually grouped together so it is easy to pick a range from dark to light for one colour.

Threading a needle

The large eyes of tapestry needles are a huge benefit when threading them, but threading several strands at once can still be tricky. If it is a real struggle, try using a larger needle.

Always keep thread length short as it will soon become worn with the friction of going back and forth through the canvas. If the thread starts to look tired always start a new thread.

A shade card makes picking the exact colour you need for your design very simple.

1 Cut two 30cm (11¾in) lengths of crewel wool. You can use the first to help measure the second.

2 Fold both threads around the eye of the needle and pinch the wool over the needle to make a crease (see inset).

3 Pull the needle out carefully, keeping the creased wool pinched between your thumb and finger.

4 Place the eye of the needle over the crease. The wool should feed through easily.

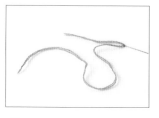

5 Knot the end. The wool is now ready to stitch.

Note

When working a large area in one colour, I find it speeds up the stitching if you thread up as many needles as possible with the same colour. These can be 'parked' in the webbing edge of your frame ready to go.

Starting and finishing a thread

This is a very important part of canvaswork. A well-stitched piece can be ruined by bulky ends on the back, or loose ends poking through to the front. Threads should always be started and finished on the front. This does mean that you often have a lot of ends at the front of the work as you stitch, which can be distracting and messy to look at, but using this method will ensure you create the best possible finish to your work.

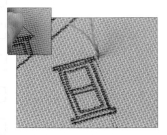

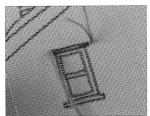

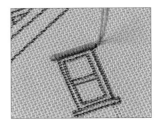

1 Within the design area, but 2.5cm (1in) away from the part on which you are working, take the needle down through the front of the canvas (see inset). Draw the yarn through so that the knot sits on the front.

2 Bring the needle up inside the area you are working, at the opposite end to the knot, and draw the yarn through.

3 Work towards the knot from the point you brought the needle up, catching the tail end of the yarn on the back as you work.

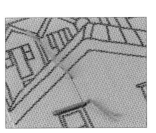

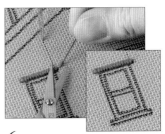

4 To finish the thread, take the needle up to the surface 2.5cm (1in) away from where you finished.

5 Use a pair of embroidery scissors to cut the thread, leaving a long tail within the design area. This will be cut off later, when you work this area of the design.

6 To remove a knot, pull the knot away from the area, then cut it. The end should spring back under the canvas, and because the tail was caught (in step 3, above), the stitching will stay secure (see inset).

Tip

Your last thread will have nowhere to be secured within the design (because it has all been worked), so turn the canvas over and thread the yarn through the backs of the other stitches. You may need to use pliers to help pull it through. Trim any excess.

SAMPLING YOUR STITCHES

Refer to the stitch section of this book (see pages 34–93) to find stitches that will suit your design. Once you have chosen your stitch – or stitches – and you have an idea about the sort of thread you would like to use, it is a good idea to test them out. It is important that the thickness of the thread is enough to cover the canvas. Generally, if the stitches within the pattern are horizontal or vertical and do not cross over, they will need more thread to cover. Diagonal stitches or crossed stitches use less thread.

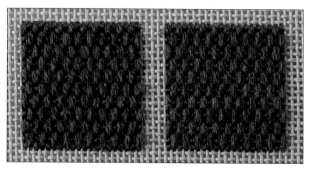

Correct (left) and too few threads (right). Note the canvas surface is visible through the test area with too few threads.

Testing your thread and stitches

Work an area of the pattern with your chosen thread. This need only be small, as you will soon see if the canvas is covered. If there is any canvas showing once you finish, add another strand of your thread. Be careful about using too many strands, as this can distort the canvas and the stitch.

How many types of stitch?

The only limit to the number of stitches you use is the size of your design. Within this example design each texture has its own stitch. The wooden panelling of the buildings all use vertical band stitches. The roofs are all tied stitches, and the doors and white wood panelling are all variations on a flat diagonal stitch.

This detail shows the stitches used in the window.

The source photograph next to the finished canvaswork picture.

Swedish Boat Houses

Within this design each texture has its own stitch. The wooden panelling of all of the buildings is worked in vertical band stitches. The main house uses fern stitch (see page 52) to represent the wooden slats of the building. This raised stitch casts a shadow, giving the building a three-dimensional appearance. The smaller houses use straight gobelin stitch (see page 59). The roofs are all tied stitches, a couching stitch is used at the front and a tied gobelin stitch (see page 60) at the back. The doors and white wood panelling are all variations of the flat diagonal stitches cashmere (see page 43), Scotch (see page 84) and mosaic (see page 47).

CHOOSING STITCHES FOR YOUR DESIGN

The choice of stitch in a canvas piece is integral to its success. But this does not mean that you have to choose a lot of stitches or very complicated stitches. Often fewer, simpler stitches work the best. Think about the complete design when choosing stitches and do a bit of planning before you begin. Remember that the plan is not set in stone and will change and adapt as you stitch, but all the areas need to work with each other. The following are a few points to consider.

Texture

Look carefully at the texture of what you are trying to represent on the canvas. Is it smooth, rough, even, uneven? Any stitches that lay flat on the canvas such as Byzantine stitch (see page 42) will give a smooth texture, while any stitches that cross over, such as Rhodes stitch (see page 81) will give a more raised appearance.

Depth

Again, any crossed stitches will give a raised appearance. The more they overlap, the greater height they will achieve. Think about what is in the foreground of the design, i.e. what is closest to the front. This will need to have the greatest height to it.

Scale

The scale of a stitch is important in portraying the dimension of a piece. Larger stitches should be used in the foreground and smaller ones for objects that are further away. Consider how much of a pattern you can fit into the area you are stitching. If the pattern has a large repeat it will not be shown if it is put into a small area. Larger patterns need some space to show them off. Scale also plays a part when the design has small detailed areas: these can only be stitched with a small scale pattern.

Stitches for background and foreground

If your design has a central object and a lot of space around it, think carefully about what stitch you will use for the background. There are two reasons for this. Firstly, you may want the background to stand out or fade away. Secondly, the speed a stitch can be worked is a big consideration in large areas. A slow stitch, such as tent stitch (see page 86), can take the enjoyment out of the piece if it takes a long time to complete.

The apple in the foreground uses fan stitch (see page 51), the only crossed stitch in the piece, as I wanted it to stand forward the most. The main direction of the stitch also slants from top left to bottom right, like all the other stitches in the design.

The next apple back in the midground uses a similar scale stitch to the red apple, but with a much flatter stitch, Scotch stitch (see page 84). The apple at the back uses a smaller variation of the same stitch to show that it is furthest away.

The background uses two different stitches. Both are flat diagonal stitches, but the one to the top of the design – Moorish stitch (see page 71) – is a smaller, more decorative stitch to give some perspective to the design. The larger stitch in the lower half is a larger variation of Scotch stitch: very quick to work and it has a less complex pattern to it.

Apples

This design uses only five stitches for the main areas – fan, Moorish and three variations of Scotch stitch (see pages 51, 71 and 84 respectively). All of them have a diagonal slant to give continuity throughout the piece, but they change in texture and scale to portray the depth of the design.

STITCH ORDER

The nature of working with canvas means that the positioning of stitches is determined by the threads and holes of the canvas. Because stitched areas should always sit next to other stitched areas and never overlap, an order of work must be established in order to create the smoothest possible outline to the shapes.

Unlike most embroidery techniques, in canvaswork you work the areas at the front of the design first and work backwards. With the example below, the bird is worked before the background as the bird is at the front. It is far easier to judge the edge of a solid area, such as the bird, than to judge the edge of a negative space, if the background was worked first.

The only exception to the rule is if there are any overstitched details in the design, such as the legs of the bird. These are much easier to site and stitch once the rest of the design is complete.

1 Draw your design on the canvas using a waterproof permanent black marker and identify the main areas. Number them in order from the front of the picture (i.e. the parts in the foreground) to the back.

1
1
2
3
4
6
7
7
6
5
6

2 Work the foreground areas in order, referring to the number sequence you made earlier.

3 With the foreground in place, fill in the background stitches, and then the final details, such as the legs.

Stitches

The following section of the book contains the instructions for a selection of stitches to introduce you to canvaswork. I have aimed to include a good variety of stitches to get any keen embroiderer started. Each stitch has written instructions, a set of diagrams and a square sample of the stitch. The contrasting area of stitches in each stitched sample demonstrates how you would work one 'row' of the repeated pattern before moving on to the next. The stitches are arranged in alphabetical order for ease of reference.

   The diagrams for each stitch show how to work an individual stitch 'block' and then how these blocks fit together to make a repeat. For many of these stitches there is more than one stage to build up a block, and these stages are shown separately from one another for clarity.

   All the stitched examples were worked on 18tpi canvas and are photographed at the same scale, so you should be able to see how they compare with each other in size.

   Before using any stitch in your work it is a good idea to sample it first on the same gauge canvas as your final piece. Seeing the stitch in scale will give you a good indication of how it will work within your design. Sampling also gives you the opportunity to make sure you are using enough strands to cover the canvas, as well as allowing you to work out how the stitch is counted, and how blocks fit together.

   Think of the illustrated stitches as a starting point. All of them can be adapted and rearranged to make new stitches. I have made some suggestions next to the stitches under 'variations' of how you could begin to make new patterns. Give these a try as well.

Note

The method for starting and finishing a thread is shown on page 27. Always use this method for the neatest results.

Working stitches

When you work a stitch adjacent to another, work into the hole used by the previous stitch, rather than out of a hole that is in use. The latter approach will catch and damage the previous stitch, while the former will result in a smooth, clean appearance. This method is not possible for all areas of a design, but try to stick to it where possible.

The area on the left-hand side of the picture is being worked incorrectly, as the thread emerges from an already-worked stitch. This will fray the yarn as you work, resulting in an untidy appearance and visible damage. On the right-hand side, you can see the needle being taken down in the correct place: any stray strands of yarn will be taken through to the back, keeping the front neat.

Raised stitches

All of the uppermost parts of the stitches in an area of cross stitches should point in the same direction (generally from bottom left to top right), as this gives a neat and tidy appearance. Compare the correctly-worked area of upright double cross stitch on the left-hand side of the picture with the incorrectly worked area on the right-hand side.

ALGERIAN EYE, VARIATION

This stitch is worked across a square of four canvas threads by four canvas threads. Begin by working eight small stitches across a single intersection of the canvas. Next, work four diagonal stitches from the four corners into the centre. Take the needle down through the centre of the square for each of these. Finally work the two horizontal and two vertical stitches, again taking the needle into the centre of the square each time.

Uses

This medium-sized stitch can be worked as a single decorative motif or as a block arranged in a grid as shown. It is a fairly flat stitch.

Variations

Instead of working the blocks as a grid, try working one vertical row and then beginning the second row two threads down, creating a half drop (see pineapple half drop stitch on page 78).

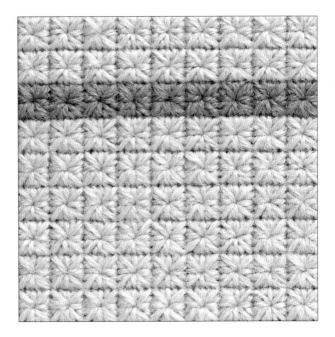

Related stitches

Algerian eye stitch is worked in a similar way, but without the initial eight small stitches. It therefore has just eight stitches in total, all taken into the centre of the square.

Eyelet stitch is again very similar, but has sixteen stitches all radiating out of the same central hole. This stitch creates more of an opening in the centre of the stitch.

Pineapple

This sampler of stitches uses an eyelet and a rococo stitch within the pineapple to give it texture. These are variations of Algerian eye and French stitch (see page 57). 21st Century. (Personal collection of Becky Hogg)

ALTERNATING CROSS

This stitch alternates a small cross with a larger cross, and the rows should interlock with each other. Begin the first row by working the small cross stitches, which cross a single intersection of the canvas and are spaced one canvas thread apart. Ensure the top thread of the cross is worked from bottom left to top right,

then work back across the row, placing the larger cross stitches between. The larger stitches are three canvas threads by one. Again ensure the top thread is always worked from bottom left to top right.

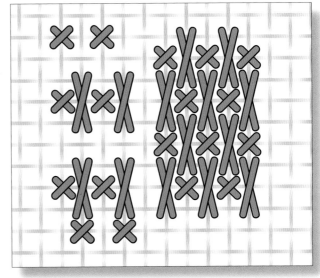

Begin working the next row by placing the small cross stitch underneath the larger cross of the previous row, then work back across the row, filling in the gaps with larger cross stitches.

Uses

At this scale, alternating cross is a small flat stitch with a lightly textured appearance.

Variations

This stitch is usually worked in horizontal rows, but it can easily be turned and worked in vertical rows.

The size of this stitch can be doubled to make a larger pattern that will cover a greater area more quickly.

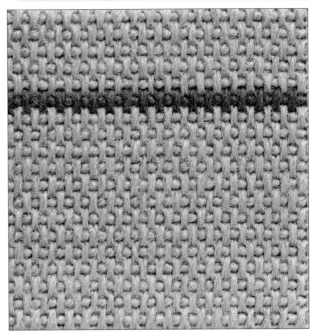

Related stitches

This stitch is also known as double cross stitch.

BARRED SQUARE

The barred square part of this stitch is contained within a grid of small cross stitches.

Work the corner cross stitches to begin. These are each across two threads by two threads of canvas. Ensure the top thread of the cross is worked bottom left to top right. Leaving a space of two threads between the crosses, work two rows of cross stitches.

Work the three vertical bars of the barred square across four canvas threads, linking one row of crosses to the next. Next, work back across each square with the horizontal bars, again across four threads of the canvas. These horizontal bars should sit next to each other.

For subsequent rows, work a further row of cross stitches first, and then fill in with the barred squares.

Uses

This is a medium-sized structured stitch with a padded appearance.

Related stitches

This stitch can be turned into woven square stitch by weaving the vertical bars of the square through the horizontal ones.

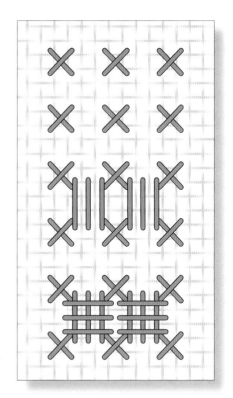

BROAD CROSS

Each broad cross of this pattern is worked across six threads by six threads of the canvas, and the pattern is worked in horizontal rows. For the first row, work three long vertical stitches next to each other, each across six threads of the canvas. Bring the needle up two threads to the left and two threads down from the top of the leftmost vertical stitch. Take a horizontal bar six threads across from this point, then work two more bars directly beneath the first.

Begin the vertical bars of the second broad cross four threads across from the vertical bars of the previous broad cross. When working the horizontal bars, ensure that they meet in the same holes as the previous broad cross in the row.

The second row of broad crosses will slot into the gaps of the first. The easiest way to place the crosses of the next row is to make the centre vertical stitch of the cross first. Place this vertical stitch first, then work a bar either side. Finally, work the horizontal bars.

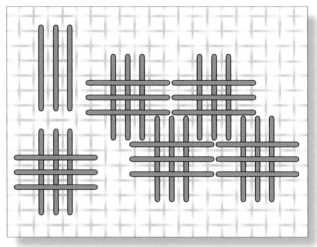

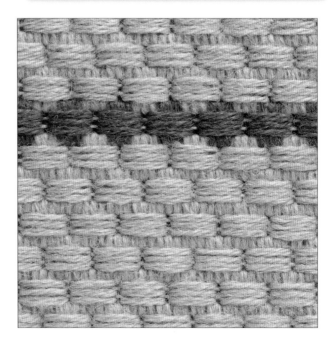

Uses

This is a medium-sized raised stitch.

Variations

The bars of this stitch can be worked in the opposite order, i.e. place the horizontal bars first, then the vertical bars.
   This stitch can be turned and worked in vertical rows.

Related stitches

Diagonal broad cross is the same stitch worked as diagonal stitches across five intersections of the canvas.

Broad cross pencil case

This pencil case was stitched using broad cross stitch. The canvas was worked as one rectangle of randomly coloured blocks. This was then made up into a pencil case. 21st century. (Author's personal collection)

BYZANTINE

This pattern is worked in long diagonal bands of the same sized stitch. Each stitch is worked from bottom left to top right across four intersections of the canvas, or four threads up and across.

Make five diagonal stitches in a vertical band. The stitch at the bottom of these will be the corner. Next, make four stitches horizontally across from the corner stitch. This will make five stitches in total for this row, the last stitch being the corner stitch.

Alternate between vertical and horizontal bands of stitches to make the stepped pattern. The second row can be worked above or below the first, fitting into the steps. The corner stitches of each row should meet.

Uses

The repeat of this stitch is quite large, which means that it covers the canvas quite quickly. It is a flat stitch and very good for backgrounds.

Variations

The size of this stitch can be varied by working over more or fewer intersections of the canvas for each stitch.

The number of stitches in each step can also be increased or decreased.

Related stitches

By alternating each row of Byzantine stitch with a row of stepped tent stitch (see page 86) the pattern becomes Jacquard stitch.

Irregular Byzantine stitch can be worked by keeping the number of stitches in each step the same, but making the stitch length in each row of the pattern change: e.g. work a row of stitches across four by four canvas threads, then three by three, then two by two etc.

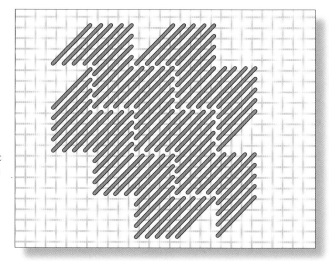

CASHMERE, DIAGONAL

Each rectangular cashmere block of this pattern is worked across two canvas threads by three. Make a tent stitch (see page 86) across one intersection of the canvas. Starting directly beneath this stitch, make a diagonal stitch across two intersections of canvas. Repeat to make a second stitch across two intersections of canvas. Finish off the rectangle with a second tent stitch at the bottom right corner of the block. To work a diagonal row, continue the pattern with two longer stitches, then a tent stitch.

This pattern is worked in diagonal rows that lean from the top left-hand corner to the bottom right-hand corner. When working the next row to the right, the first tent stitch of each cashmere block should meet the top right hand corner of the previous row's cashmere blocks.

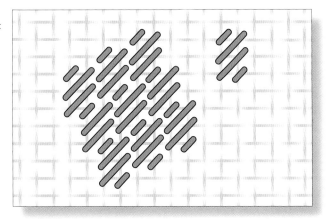

Uses

This is a flat stitch with a small pattern repeat. It is very good for backgrounds.

Variations

The cashmere block can be turned ninety degrees and work as a diagonal band with a shallow slant.

The angle of the block itself can be reversed so that each stitch is made from the bottom right to the top left. The step pattern will then travel from bottom left to top right.

The cashmere block can be alternated with six tent stitches (see chequer stitch on page 45).

Related stitches

Straight cashmere stitch uses the complete cashmere block in straight horizontal and vertical rows. This pattern forms a straight grid of rectangles. Each block of this stitch can be alternately reversed (see reversed cushion on page 47).

CHAIN

This is worked as long straight rows that start at the top and are stitched down to the bottom of the design. The finished stitch resembles a chain, hence the name.

Begin by bringing the needle up through a hole of the canvas, and take it back down through the same hole, without pulling the thread tight, in order to leave a loose loop on the front of the canvas. Next, bring the needle up two canvas threads below the first part of the stitch and through the loose loop left on the canvas. Now the thread can be pulled tight. Repeat the stitch by taking the needle back down through the same hole it has just come up (through the first loop) and out again two threads below.

At the end of a row make a small vertical stitch over one canvas thread to hold the final loop in place. The second row of chain should be worked one thread across from the first.

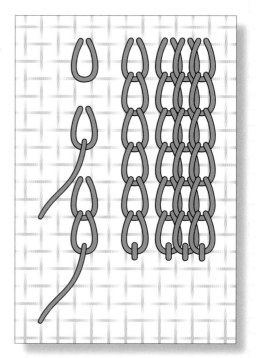

Uses

This is a small, flat stitch and useful for narrow shapes. It is also very slow to work, so only use it for small areas.

Variations

The length of the chain can vary, although the longer you make it the more likely it is that canvas will show.

The second row can be started one canvas thread down, to give the design a half drop.

Related stitches

Detached chain stitch is a single chain loop held by a small vertical stitch (like the last stitch of a row). These can be worked as rows or as individual stitches.

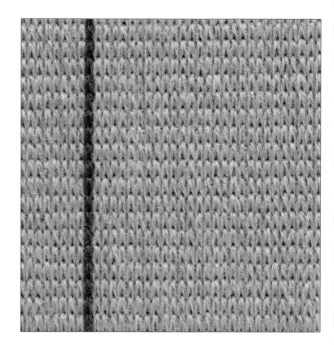

CHEQUER

This chequerboard stitch is made up of two alternating stitch blocks of tent stitch (see page 86) and cushion stitch (see page 47). The cushion stitch is made of seven diagonal stitches, covering a square of four by four canvas threads.

Begin with a tent stitch in the top left-hand corner, then make a stitch across two canvas intersections, then three, then four, then three, then two and finally another tent stitch. Directly next to this make a square of sixteen tent stitches (i.e. four by four).

Continue with these two blocks across a horizontal row. On the row below, place the tent stitch block under the cushion block and the cushion block under the tent block. Make sure all of the stitches angle from the bottom left to the top right.

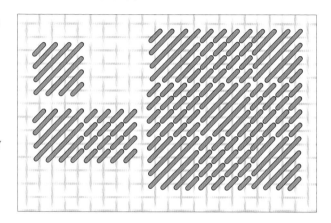

Uses

This is a flat stitch with a fairly large pattern repeat, which makes it good for large areas such as backgrounds. It is slower to work than other flat stitches due to the tent stitch.

Variations

This stitch can also be worked with a cashmere stitch (see page 43) in place of the cushion stitch, in which case alternate with blocks of six tent stitches.

CUSHION, CROSSED

The cushion stitch block is made of seven diagonal stitches, covering a square of four by four canvas threads. Begin with a tent stitch (see page 86) in the top left-hand corner. Next, make a stitch across two canvas intersections, then three, then four, then three, then two and finally another tent stitch to complete the block.

With the cushion stitch block in place, work the crossed part of the stitch. This is worked in the same way as half a cushion stitch block over the top of the first, but worked in the opposite direction. Begin with a long stitch across the centre of the block from top left to bottom right. Below and to the left of this long stitch, work another three stitches: the first across three canvas intersections, the second across then two intesections and finally across a single intersection.

This crossed block can be repeated horizontally in rows or as an individual block.

Uses

A flat stitch with a medium-sized pattern repeat, crossed cushion is good for more decorative backgrounds.

Variations

The cushion stitch block can be slanted in alternate directions (see cushion, reversed on the opposite page), in which case the crossed stitches should also be alternated.

The size of the cushion block can be increased or decreased. Blocks of differently sized crossed cushion work well together.

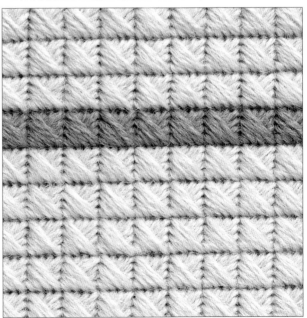

CUSHION, REVERSED

This version of cushion stitch is worked in straight rows. Each cushion block is made up of five diagonal stitches across a square of three by three canvas threads. Begin with a tent stitch (see page 86) in the top left-hand corner. Then make a stitch across two canvas intersections, then three, then two and finally make another tent stitch.

For the next block to the right, reverse the stitch direction: begin at the bottom left-hand side with a reversed tent stitch and work the other four stitches across to the top right-hand corner. The row below should mirror the row above.

Uses

Reversed cushion is a slightly raised, structured stitch with a small pattern repeat. This adds a subtle texture to a piece.

Variations

This stitch can be increased in size for a different effect.

Related stitches

This stitch is also known as Scotch or Scottish stitch.

When the stitch direction is the same for all of the blocks it is simply called cushion stitch.

When the cushion block is reduced to just three stitches, the stitch becomes reversed mosaic stitch.

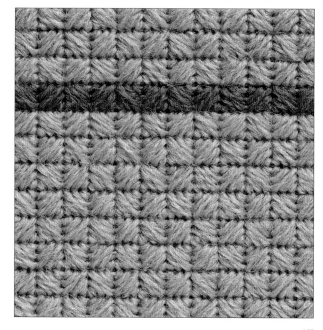

DOUBLE LINKED CROSS

This stitch is made of two crossed blocks, linked together.
Each pair is worked together. Make two cross stitches next to
each other, each across two by two threads of the canvas. Make
sure the top stitch of each runs from bottom left to top right.
Next, make a vertical stitch across each. Finally make one long
horizontal stitch across both crosses (i.e. across four canvas
threads) to complete the block.

Work the blocks in horizontal rows. The row beneath should
start two canvas threads across to give the pattern a bricked look.

Uses

A small, raised stitch with a
medium-sized pattern repeat.
Great texture and very brick
like, but slow to work.

Variations

The blocks can be worked
vertically, and more blocks
can be linked together. The
pattern can also be worked in
straight vertical rows, without
the bricking.

Related stitches

This stitch is also called
leviathan linked or
Smyrna linked.

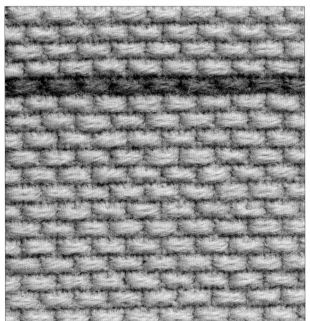

48

DOUBLE STRAIGHT CROSS

This stitch is made up of a large cross stitch held down by a smaller one. Make a horizontal stitch across four canvas threads, then make a vertical stitch of the same length across the middle of it. Next, make a diagonal stitch across the centre of this cross, covering two canvas intersections from top left to bottom right. Finally, make another diagonal stitch of the same length from bottom left to top right. Work the crosses in horizontal rows. The next stitch to the right should join at the left-hand edge of the previous cross.

The next row is worked below the first, two canvas threads down and across, so that the crosses fit into the gaps of the previous row. Make sure that the top stitch on all the crosses is always bottom left to top right.

Uses

A great bumpy small raised stitch, double straight cross can be worked as an individual stitch. It is good for creating a textured area.

Related stitches

This stitch is also known as star stitch.

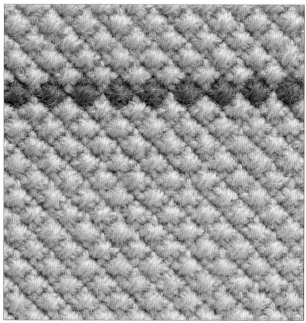

DUTCH

This crossed stitch is made up of an oblong cross stitch over a straight stitch. To start, make a vertical stitch across four threads of the canvas, then come down one thread and across two to the left of the top of this stitch. Make a diagonal stitch across four threads and down two threads of the canvas. Go up two canvas threads and make a diagonal stitch across four threads and down two. Work the pattern in horizontal rows so that the edges of the crosses touch.

The row below should fit into the gaps of the first, touching at the corners of the cross.

Uses

A bumpy, raised, medium-sized stitch that is good for adding texture.

Variations

The vertical stitch can be worked last rather than first.

The stitch can also be turned so that the rows are worked vertically.

FAN

This square stitch is worked across three by three canvas threads and is made up of seven stitches. Begin with a vertical straight stitch across three threads of canvas, working from bottom to top. Bring the needle out one thread across from the bottom of this stitch and take it into the same hole at the top. Repeat this 'fanning' around the square, each time taking the needle into the same hole. The pattern can be worked in vertical or horizontal bands. Make sure the seven stitches are always worked in the same order (i.e. the fan always follows the same direction).

Uses

This is a fairly smooth small stitch. It is quite slow to work, but you can give direction to an area by angling the fan in the appropriate direction.

Variations

Try alternating the direction of the fan for each row, or alternating each fan within a row.

Related stitches

This stitch is also known as ray stitch.

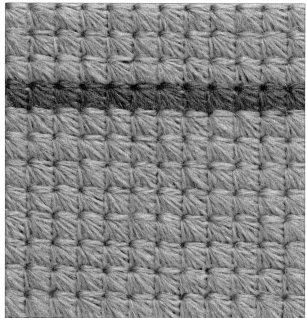

FERN

Fern stitch is an overlapping band stitch that is always worked
in the same direction. Make a diagonal stitch across two
intersections of the canvas from top left to bottom right. Take the
needle under one thread of the canvas to the left and back to the
surface. Make a second diagonal stitch across two intersections of
the canvas, ending three canvas threads across from the start of the
first stitch. Take the needle across the back of the stitch and out
one thread underneath the first
stitch. Repeat the two diagonal
stitches, each one a canvas
thread beneath the last.

The next vertical row is
started from the top again and
worked down, meeting the
previous row at the edge.

Uses

A very straight band stitch,
fern is very good for clearly
defined stripes.

Variations

The stitch can vary in length
and angle. By making the
diagonal stitch across three
threads and down one, for
example, the angle of the
stitch can be made
considerably shallower.

Alternate rows could be
worked top to bottom then
bottom to top for a different
final appearance.

FISHBONE, STEPPED

This stitch is made up of alternate rows of the same crossed stitch turned horizontally and vertically. Begin with a vertical straight stitch over four threads of the canvas. Cross this stitch at the bottom with a horizontal stitch across two threads of the canvas. Start the next long vertical stitch one thread up and across to the right from the first. Again cross it, with a horizontal stitch across two threads of the canvas. When enough vertical stitches have been worked, begin a horizontal row.

For the horizontal row below the first vertical row, make a horizontal stitch across four threads of the canvas, ending it at the bottom point of the last vertical stitch. Cross this stitch to the right-hand side of the horizontal stitch. Working down and across one canvas thread to the left at a time, work a row of horizontal stitches.

Continue alternating between vertical and horizontal stitch rows.

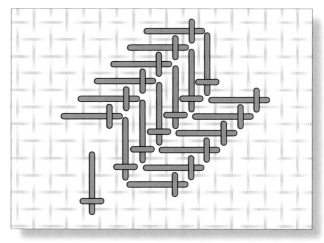

Uses

A slightly raised band stitch, stepped fishbone is ideal for filling an area with a clear diagonal line.

Variations

The length of the long stitch can vary from row to row.

Related stitches

Horizontal fishbone stitch can be produced by working just the rows of horizontal fishbone stitches and joining them in diagonal rows.

FLORENTINE

Florentine stitch is made up of a series of straight stitches of equal length, rising and falling in a pattern of steps.

In this example, each stitch is made across four threads of the canvas, and each step across the pattern is two threads of the canvas above or below the previous stitch. By varying the number of stitches at each step of the design a pattern of waves is produced. The pattern is set by the first complete wave of stitches. Each row above or below this then repeats the same design.

Generally one colour is used for one complete wave of the design. A varied use of colour is essential for this stitch.

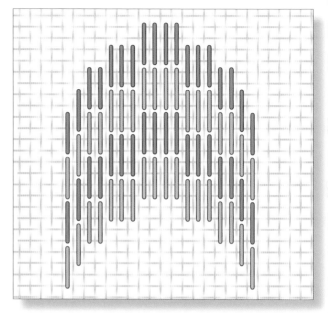

Uses

This stitch needs a large area to display its pattern.

Variations

The illustrated design is a very basic example of the stitch, which has endless variations.

Related stitches

This stitch is also known as flame stitch or Bargello work.

Icicles

The background of this piece uses diagonal stitches which have blended together effortlessly.
20th century. (Personal collection of Heather Lewis)

FLYING CROSS

Flying cross stitch is a slightly elongated cross stitch, that is worked in diagonal rows. Each cross stitch is made across two by three threads of the canvas.

Making sure that the top stitch is worked from bottom left to top right, make one cross stitch, and then bring your needle up one canvas thread below the top right-hand corner of this stitch. Start your second cross from here. This and every following cross should start one canvas thread below the previous cross.

Work the second row directly beneath the first.

Uses

This is a medium-sized stitch with a slightly raised effect that is useful for filling in large areas where some texture is required.

Variations

The crosses could be turned lengthways to give a shallower diagonal stripe.

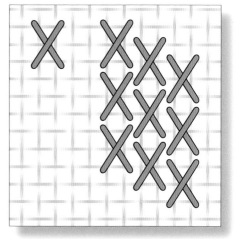

FRENCH

This stitch is worked across four threads of canvas by two. Make a vertical stitch across four threads of canvas, but do not pull it too tight. Bring the needle up to the left of the stitch, two threads down and one thread across. Make a horizontal holding stitch across one thread of the canvas, anchoring the long stitch to the left. Make a second vertical stitch in the same holes as the first. This time make a small stitch anchoring it to the right. Work a row of these stitches, beginning the stitch two canvas threads across each time.

For the second row, begin the vertical stitch in the same canvas hole as the small horizontal stitches of the row above. The pairs of stitches should fit into the spaces left by the previous row.

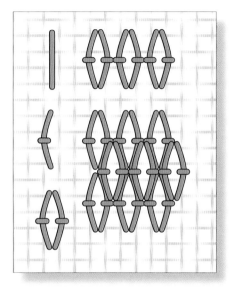

Uses

This is a small, delicate and flat pattern that will fit into a small area. Note that French stitch can be quite slow to work.

Variations

The length of the vertical stitch can be increased, as long as it is across an even number of threads.

Related stitches

Rococo stitch is a slightly larger version of the same stitch. Work a French stitch, then make a third vertical stitch, again into the same two holes of the canvas, and anchor this just to the left of the first two stitches. Make a fourth vertical stitch and anchor this to the right.

Rococo stitch is worked in rows that slot into each other in exactly the same way as French stitch.

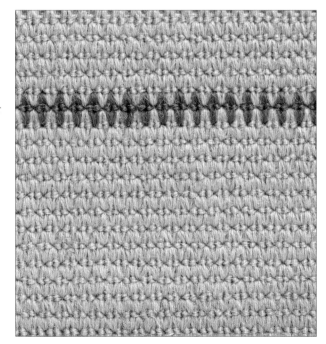

GOBELIN, ENCROACHING

This stitch is working in horizontal bands of slanted stitches. Start by making a row of stitches, each of which is worked over five threads by one thread of the canvas.

Begin the second row four threads below the first, and again make a row of stitches each over five threads by one thread, allowing for the encroachment of one thread between rows. Always take the needle into the previous row, between stitches.

Do not bring the needle out of the previous row as this can disturb the lay of the stitches. The rows of this stitch must be worked either from top to bottom or bottom to top in the area to be covered.

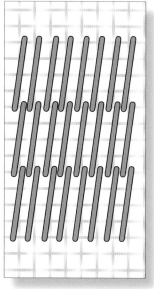

Uses

The rows of this stitch are quite wide, making this a fairly large pattern. This makes encroaching gobelin good for quickly filling large areas.

Variations

The depth of this stitch can be altered, making a smaller, tighter band. The stitch depth can be altered within a row to create a more random texture.

Related stitches

The same stitch can be worked without the encroachment in a variation called slanted gobelin. Each following row is worked into the same holes at the bottom of the previous row.

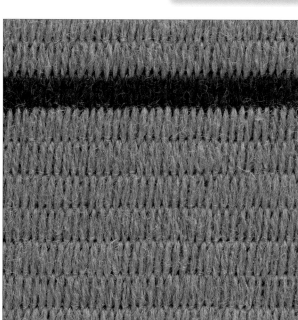

GOBELIN, STRAIGHT

This is a straight stitch worked over a horizontal padding stitch. Start by making a padding stitch across the width of the area to be covered. Work back over this, adding vertical stitches across two threads of the canvas.

Start the padding of the second row two canvas threads below the first padding stitch. Work back across this, working each vertical stitch into the same hole of the previous row of stitches. Always take the needle down into the occupied canvas hole, not out of it.

Uses

This is a neat small stitch, with a slightly padded appearance. It is good for small striped areas.

Variations

The length of the straight stitches can be increased, in which case more rows of padding stitch are needed. If the stitch were across three threads of canvas, two rows of padding stitches would be laid first, for example.

This stitch can also be worked without the padding.

Related stitches

This stitch is also called upright gobelin.

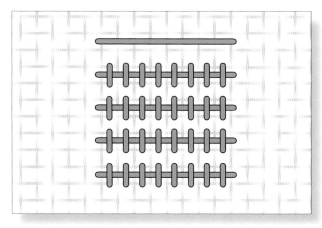

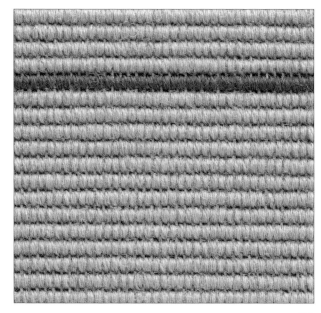

GOBELIN, TIED

This stitch is made up of bands of slanted stitches held down (tied) in the centre.

To begin, make a slanted stitch across three by one canvas threads. Make a reversed tent stitch in the centre of this. Repeat across the row, always making the long stitch first and then cross it.

On each following row, begin two threads down and make the long stitch so that it encroaches into the previous row, sharing the canvas hole with the reversed tent stitch. Always work the rows from top to bottom or bottom to top of an area.

Uses

This is a very small and neat stitch that can give a delicate texture to small areas. Tied gobelin is very slow to work.

Variations

Try turning the stitch through ninety degrees to work vertical bands.

Related stitches

This stitch is also known as knotted stitch.

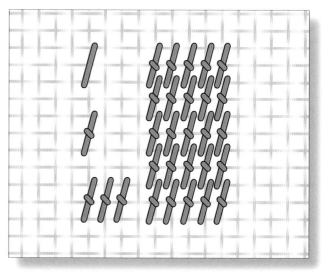

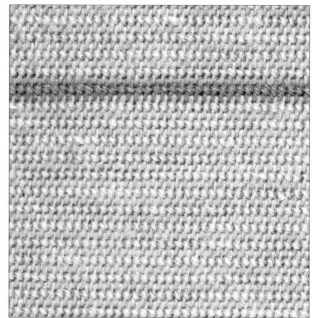

HALF RHODES

Each half Rhodes stitch is worked in a square of six by six canvas threads. Begin by making a long stitch across six diagonal intersections of the canvas, from bottom left to top right. Work the next and each following stitch from the bottom to the top, in order to keep an even tension on the stitch.

Bring the needle out one thread to the right from the bottom corner and take it up to one thread to the left of the top corner. Repeat the process for the third stitch. The fourth stitch should be vertical. Make three more stitches, so that the last stitch starts and ends in line with the first stitch.

Begin the second stitch six canvas threads below the first, so that the two stitches meet along their flat edges.

To begin the second vertical row to the right, begin three threads down and two threads in to the right of the lowest half Rhodes stitch. The hourglass shapes of the stitches should interlock together.

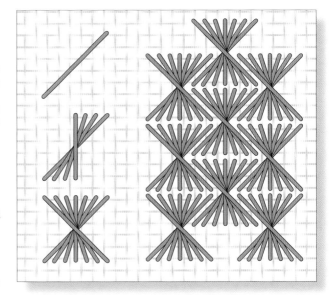

Uses

This is a large, highly raised stitch that is fantastic for adding texture.

Variations

This stitch can be worked as a single motif as well as part of a pattern.

If the first and third rows of the pattern are worked without a gap between them, a diamond shape is left between the rows. This can be filled with a suitable motif, such as eyelet stitch (see page 37) or tent stitch (see page 86).

HUNGARIAN GROUNDING

This two part wavy stitch is made up of vertical stitches of different lengths. For the first row, all the stitches are across four threads of canvas. Begin by making the first vertical stitch. Make the next stitch across one thread to the right and move it up one canvas thread. Repeat for the third stitch. The fourth stitch is down one canvas thread. Repeat for the next stitch. Continue in this pattern for the width of the area.

For the second row, all the stitches are across two threads of canvas. Directly under the highest stitch in the first row make a stitch. Then make one to either side of this, again directly under the row above. Finally make a fourth stitch under the first of this group, to make a diamond.

With two canvas threads spacing between each, repeat the diamond pattern across the row.

Next, make a row like the first, mirroring it below the diamonds (note: the first and every following fourth long stitch should touch the previous row, containing the diamond between).

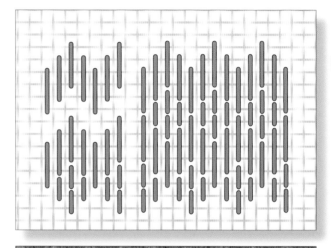

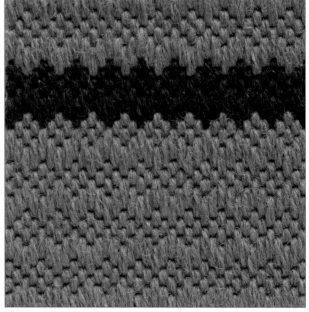

Uses

This is a decorative flat stitch that works well for backgrounds.

Variations

Using different colours for the two parts of the stitch works well. The diamond part of the stitch can be worked as three stitches instead of four. Simply make the two centre stitches into one, across four threads.

Related stitches

Worked without the row of long stitches, the diamond part of the stitch (when worked as three stitches, instead of four) is Hungarian stitch. Work these with two canvas threads between each as shown, and on the following row fit the same stitches into the spaces left.

The Swamp

This design uses horizontal stitches to recreate the surface of the water. Multiple colours were mixed in the needle to give a painted look to the piece. The grasses at the front were stitched over the surface of the canvaswork with a sharp needle. 21st century. (Personal collection of Paola Bianchi)

Berlin wool work

This small piece of canvaswork includes plush work in the central flowers, and also bead work. Late 19th or early 20th Century. (RSN Collection)

JOHN

This stitch is made up of blocks of tent (see page 86) and reversed tent stitch with a long stitch separating them.

First work three tent stitches in a vertical row. To the left of these, work three reversed tent stitches to make a rectangular block.

Beneath this block make a stitch across two by one threads of canvas from top left to bottom right. Repeat this group in vertical rows.

Uses

This is a small neat stitch with a slight texture.

Variations

Try beginning each vertical row one canvas thread higher each time. This will give a stepped effect.

Related stitches

Without the longer stitch to break up the blocks, this stitch becomes alternating tent.

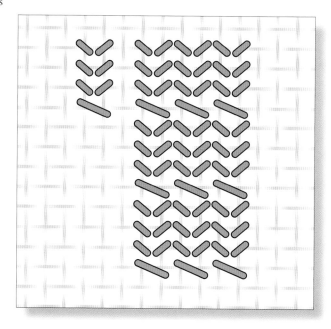

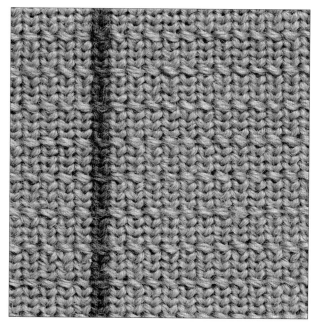

LEAF

Begin with a slanted stitch across one and down three canvas threads. Make a second slanted stitch to mirror the first, into the same hole. Beginning one thread above the previous stitches, make a straight stitch over four canvas threads and down into the same canvas hole as the previous two stitches.

Now work the right-hand side of the leaf. Come up one intersection down and across from the top end of the slanted stitch and take the needle down one canvas thread below the lower centre point of the leaf (the hole below the one shared by the first three stitches). Next, bring the needle up a further canvas intersection down and across from this stitch and make a stitch across three canvas intersections. Make two similar stitches below the first in the same way.

Work the left-hand side of the leaf in the same way. Work in horizontal rows, fitting the next row into the spaces of the first. For positioning of the stitch it is easiest to work the rows top to bottom. Make sure that you tuck the ends of the stitches under the last stitch of the previous row.

Opposite
Owl

This piece shows off the leaf stitch in the background by varying the colour of each leaf. 21st century. (Personal collection of Kate Haxell)

Uses

Leaf stitch creates a large stitch motif that can be worked alone or as a pattern. It is particularly good for large foliage and texture.

Variations

A vertical straight stitch can be worked across the centre of the leaf to give it a vein.

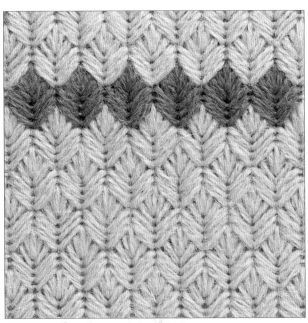

Horse Chestnut

A canvas stitch sampler with a wide variety of stitches in it. The leaf to the right uses a variation of Florentine stitch (see page 54) to show the direction of the veins. 20th Century. (Personal collection of Jean Panter)

MALTESE CROSS

The cross is worked in two overlapping parts. First, make a diagonal stitch from the bottom left-hand side to the top right-hand side across four and up eight canvas threads. Return to the bottom, one canvas thread across to the right, and take this stitch up to one thread to the left of the top corner. Next, make a third stitch; this one should be vertical across eight threads. Then make a fourth and fifth stitch following the pattern, ending up directly above and below the first stitch.

To make the second part of the cross, bring the needle up two threads across to the left and down two threads from the top left-hand corner. Make a diagonal stitch down to the right, ending two threads up and across from the lower corner of the first part of the cross. Return to the left, one thread down from the start of the previous stitch and take the thread across to one thread up from the previous stitch. Make a third horizontal stitch, then a fourth and fifth stitch following the pattern, so that the final stitch is from bottom left to top right.

Work the crosses in horizontal rows, so that their flat ends touch. The following rows fit into the spaces left, so that the centre top of the next cross meets the lower corner of the join of the crosses above.

Uses

Maltese cross produces a very large raised motif that can be used alone or as part of a pattern. It is a fairly quick stitch to work and can be used in large areas where a very raised texture is needed.

MILANESE

This stitch is worked in diagonal rows of triangular units. For the first unit, make a tent stitch across one canvas intersection. Below it make a stitch across two canvas intersections, then three, then four. Repeat this sequence of stitches over one, two, three and four canvas intersections in a diagonal row from top left to bottom right.

Work the next row of triangles in reverse, so that they fit into the gaps of the first row. The smallest stitch of one row should always be next to the largest stitch of the following row.

Uses

Milanese stitch gives a flat, medium-sized pattern repeat which fills in quickly. It is good for backgrounds.

Related stitches

The triangles of this stitch can also be made with horizontal stitches across two, four, six and eight threads of the canvas to make straight Milanese stitch. This stitch has straight vertical bands of the pattern.

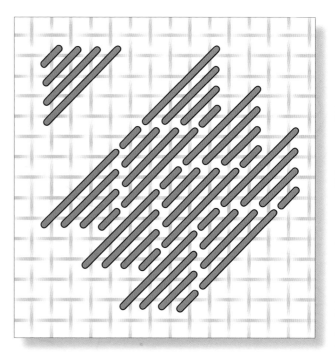

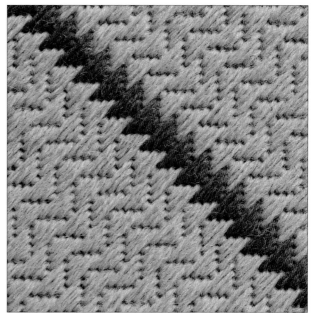

MOORISH

This stitch is worked in diagonal rows and is very similar to Scotch stitch (see page 84).

To begin, a row of interlocking squares is worked. Make a tent stitch across one intersection of the canvas, then below it make successive stitches across two, three, two then one intersection again. Repeat these stitches to produce a diagonal pattern of interlocking squares across the area being worked.

Adjacent to the squares, work a row of tent stitches following the step of the squares. These should be three tent stitches up and three tent stitches across. Next, work back down the other side of the tent stitches, fitting the square pattern into the spaces. Repeat these two rows to continue the pattern.

Uses

This is slightly more textured version of Scotch stitch. It is good for backgrounds and filling areas quite quickly.

The pattern gives a nice diagonal stripe.

Related stitches

Try working rows of cashmere stitch (see page 43) instead of Scotch stitch for the interlocking squares. Intersperse the rows with tent stitch as described above.

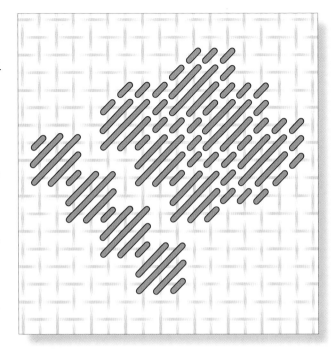

NORWICH

This very large square stitch is worked across a section of canvas measuring nine threads by nine threads. Begin with a stitch from the bottom left-hand corner to the top right-hand corner across nine intersections of the canvas (1–2). Then make a stitch from the bottom right-hand corner to the top left-hand corner (3–4). Continue to follow the numbers on the stitch diagram to the right – you will make eighteen stitches in total. The final stitch (35–36), should be slipped under stitch 29–30 at the edge.

Uses

This stitch can be worked as a single motif or as part of a block of the same stitch.

Variations

The same stitch can be worked across any square of an uneven number of threads. A combination of sizes in one area can work well.

Related stitches

This stitch is also known as waffle stitch.

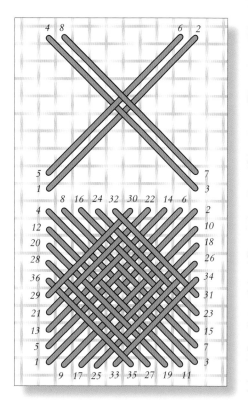

OATMEAL

This stitch combines two different sizes of diagonal square stitches, which are worked at opposite angles to each other.

Begin by working a diagonal row of interlocking square stitches. Make a tent stitch across one intersection of the canvas, then below it make stitches across two, three, four, three, two then one intersection again. Repeat this pattern across the diagonal of the area being worked.

Once this row is complete make the smaller square stitches in the spaces. These begin with a reversed tent stitch, then a stitch across two, three, two then one intersection of the canvas. Repeat these along the row. The longest of the stitches should touch at the corners.

The next row is a repeat of the first. The longest stitches of these squares should touch the longest stitches of the previous row of large diagonal squares.

Uses

The two different directions of the stitches in this pattern give it an interesting texture. Oatmeal stitch has a fairly large pattern repeat, but it is good for backgrounds.

Variations

This stitch carefully interlocks two different stitches together. There are many stitches that follow this diagonal design and could be put together. For example, the smaller square could be replaced with a fan stitch (see page 51).

OBLONG DOUBLE TIED CROSS

This stitch is worked in bands of oblong crosses. First, make an oblong cross stitch across two by five canvas threads. Always make the top stitch bottom left to top right. Next, tie it twice in the centre with two horizontal stitches across two threads of canvas. Make the next cross and again tie it in the centre. Repeat across the row. Work the next row directly beneath the first.

Uses

Oblong double-tied cross is a fairly large raised stitch with a definite horizontal striped effect.

Variations

The rows could be worked vertically.
After working the first cross, the second could begin two canvas threads down, giving a diagonal stepped effect.

Related stitches

Without the tying stitches this is just oblong cross stitch. Worked across three vertical threads and tied just once in the middle the stitch becomes oblong tied cross stitch.

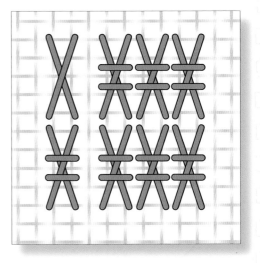

PARISIAN

This simple stitch is worked in horizontal bands. Make a vertical stitch across two threads of canvas. Next to it, make a vertical stitch across four threads of canvas. Repeat these two stitches alternating between two and four threads of canvas.

For the second row, place the small stitch directly below the longer stitch and vice versa. Repeat on each following row.

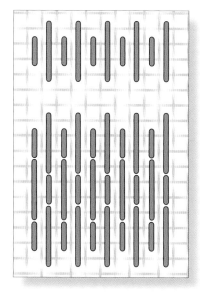

Uses

Parisian is a medium-sized flat stitch which fills in areas quickly. It is good for slightly textured backgrounds.

Variations

To work a smaller version of the stitch, stitch across one and three threads of the canvas. Parisian stitch can also be worked in vertical bands.

Related stitches

If worked diagonally, by alternating the stitches across one and two intersections of the canvas, the stitch becomes condensed mosaic stitch.

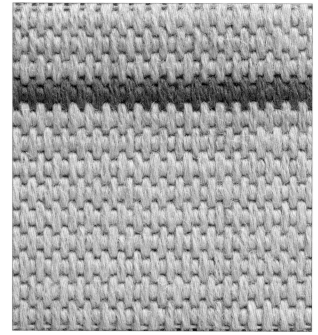

PAVILION, TIED

This is a large diamond-shaped pattern made up of vertical stitches. Make the tied central stitch of the diamond first. This is a long vertical stitch across eight canvas threads, tied in the centre with a horizontal stitch across two canvas threads. With this in place, start to fill in the diamond shape with two vertical stitches, each over six canvas threads, to either side of the tied central stitch. Next, add vertical stitches over four canvas threads on both sides and finally add vertical stitches over two canvas threads at the edges.

Work the pattern in horizontal rows, beginning at the top of the next diamond eight threads across from the top of the previous diamond.

Uses

This is a large flat stitch that covers the canvas quickly.

Variations

The stitch can be worked without the tie.

A smaller diamond pattern can be worked with five stitches rather than seven, the first over six canvas threads.

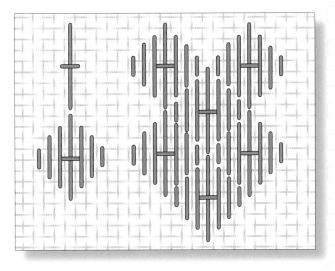

PERSPECTIVE, VARIATION

This is an overlapping stitch, worked in horizontal bands. The rows of this stitch must always be worked from top to bottom.

Make a diagonal stitch across two intersections of canvas, from top left to bottom right. Make two more in the same way directly underneath the first. To the right of these, make three diagonal stitches that angle from bottom left to top right to meet the first three. Repeat this six stitch chevron pattern horizontally across the area to be worked, leaving no gaps between.

For the row below, the chevrons are repeated, but rather than point down, they now point up. Where the six chevron stitches above meet in a downward point, the same canvas holes are used for the upward point of the chevron stitch below. Complete the row in the same way.

The third row will be the same as the first. Continue the rows alternating the direction of the chevron.

Uses

A medium-sized decorative stitch with good texture.

Related stitches

For perspective stitch, work twelve stitches in each chevron (i.e. six stitches and six stitches) and overlap only the bottom three stitches of each row.

PINEAPPLE HALF DROP

This stitch is worked in vertical rows of crossed blocks of pineapple stitch, with a half drop to each row.

Make four vertical stitches across four threads of canvas to make a block. Next, bring the needle up one thread across from the top left-hand corner and take it down one thread across from the bottom right-hand corner. Make a second diagonal stitch across the block from the bottom left-hand corner to the top right-hand corner. Always make the top stitch of the cross in the same direction. Tie down the cross with a vertical stitch across the centre of the cross and over one vertical canvas thread. Make the next block in the same way directly beneath the first, and continue in a vertical row.

For the next row to the right, begin the block two threads above the lower right-hand corner of the last block. The cross of the next row should tuck under the vertical edge of the previous row.

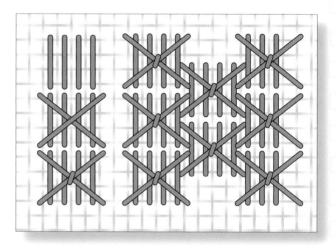

Uses

This is a medium- to large-sized stitch with a lot of texture and a fairly raised appearance. It can be used individually as a single motif.

Related stitches

This stitch can be worked in vertical or horizontal rows to make a grid. The stitch then becomes pineapple stitch.

Note that the corners of the crosses should meet for pineapple stitch, and this leaves a small gap between the blocks.

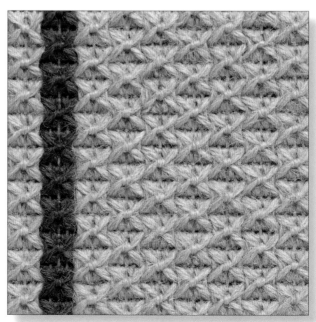

PLAIT

This is a heavy horizontal stitch that looks like a row of plaited braid. All the stitches on the reverse of the canvas should be vertical. Make a diagonal stitch from bottom left to top right across four intersections of canvas. Bring the needle out four canvas threads below the top corner of this stitch, then make a diagonal stitch up four and across two threads of canvas to the left. Bring the needle out vertically below the end of this stitch.

Repeat these two stitches across the band of the plait. The following rows should be worked in the same direction as the first (i.e. left to right).

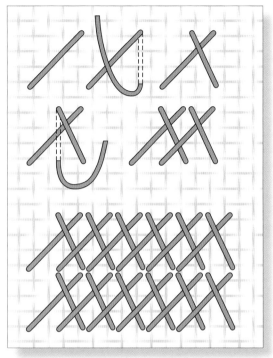

Uses

This stitch gives a firm raised band of pattern and fills in quickly.

Variations

For a smaller plait, work the band across two horizontal threads of canvas, making the first stitch across two intersections of canvas.

Related stitches

This stitch is also called Spanish plait stitch.

Algerian plait stitch is identical in appearance to plait stitch on the front of the canvas, but on the reverse has horizontal stitches. It is worked like a herringbone stitch: after the first stitch is made, take the needle back across two vertical threads of the canvas to the left.

Make a second stitch that crosses the first and again take the needle back across two vertical threads of the canvas to the left. Continue across the band of the plait.

RAISED SPOT

This is a very dense stitch, best worked with several threads in the needle at once. Make a vertical stitch across three threads of the canvas, then repeat the stitch through the same holes several times, until you can not get any more thread through. Make a note of how many times you are wrapping around each stitch and keep this consistent throughout.

Move two canvas threads to the right and repeat to make the next stitch, making sure to match the number of times you wrap around each stitch. The second row fits into the gaps of the first, encroaching by one canvas thread.

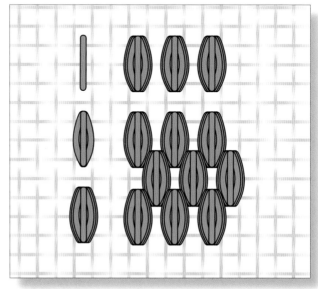

Uses

This is a raised small stitch that gives great texture. It is very slow to work.

Variations

The stitch can be made smaller or larger and can vary within the area being worked to create a more random texture.

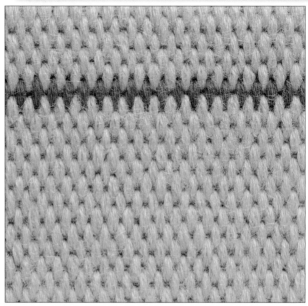

RHODES

This stitch is made up of raised squares worked in a grid pattern. Each completed square measures six threads by six threads of canvas.

Begin one canvas thread in from the bottom left-hand corner and take this over to one thread in from the top right-hand corner of the complete square (i.e. across four threads and up six threads of the canvas).

Return to the bottom edge and make a stitch one thread to the right of the first and one thread to the left of the top edge of the first stitch. Continue in an anti-clockwise direction around the square fanning the stitches. The sixth stitch should be from the bottom right-hand corner to the top left-hand corner.

Continue around the square until twelve stitches have been made. The last of these should be from the top right-hand corner to the bottom left-hand corner. Move to the next square, either below or across.

Always work the stitches in the same order and direction, so that the last stitch is always the same.

Uses

This is a very raised large stitch, and it creates a strong textured grid.

Variations

The same stitch can be worked at any size, smaller or larger. A combination of sizes can work well together.

If the stitch is made much larger, a single tent stitch can be placed in the centre to hold the long final stitch in place.

RICE

This is a large cross stitch with a cross over each of its corners. Begin by making a cross stitch across four by four threads of the canvas. Make sure that the top stitch is always bottom left to top right. Now beginning at the top left-hand corner make a diagonal stitch across two intersections of canvas, crossing the corner of the first cross. Repeat at each corner, so that these stitches meet at the centre points of the sides of the cross. Repeat the rice stitch block in horizontal rows.

Uses

This is a good basic medium-sized stitch. It is a little raised and has an even-textured appearance. It can be used as a single motif or as part of a pattern.

Variations

Rice stitch can be worked larger or smaller, as long as it is across a square of any number of even threads.

Related stitches

This stitch is also known as crossed corners.

When worked with horizontal and vertical stitches, it produces a diamond-shaped pattern called straight rice stitch. To produce this, make an upright cross over four threads of canvas, then cross the corners across two threads of canvas.

ROMANIAN COUCHING

This stitch uses small diagonal stitches to hold down one long stitch. Make a long horizontal stitch across the area to be couched from left to right. Bring the needle up two canvas threads to the left of the end of the first stitch. Make a diagonal stitch from the bottom right to the top left, across the long stitch and holding it to one horizontal canvas thread. Next, miss two vertical canvas threads then make the second diagonal stitch. Continue across the width of the first stitch holding it down at these intervals.

For the next row, make a second long stitch under the first and work back across it, placing diagonal stitches directly beneath those of the first row. Always work this stitch from top to bottom.

Uses

This is a quick stitch that covers smoothly and gives a lightly textured surface.

Variations

Try keeping the length of the holding stitch consistent (two threads by one, in this example) but varying its position. You could brick the holding stitches on successive rows, or make some closer together or further apart.

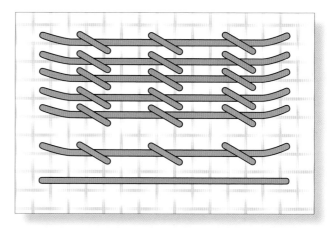

Related stitches

When the laid thread is held down with a single reversed tent stitch this becomes Bokhara couching. Place the holding stitches three threads apart and brick the pattern on the second row.

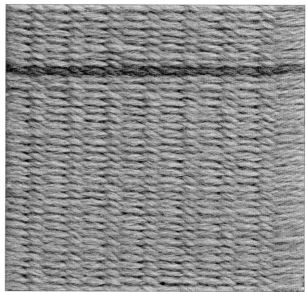

SCOTCH

This is a diagonal stitch made of interlocking squares. Make a tent stitch across one canvas intersection. Below it make a stitch across two canvas intersections, then further stitches across three, two and one canvas intersections. This makes the first square.

Repeat the sequence diagonally: across one, two, three, two, one, two, three, two etc. Continue in diagonal rows. The shortest stitch of the next row will sit next to the longest stitch of the previous row and vice versa, so the second row should interlock with the spaces of the first.

Uses

This is a flat medium-sized stitch that fills in quite quickly.

Variations

The size of the square in this stitch can be increased or reduced.

Related stitches

This stitch is also known as condensed cushion stitch.

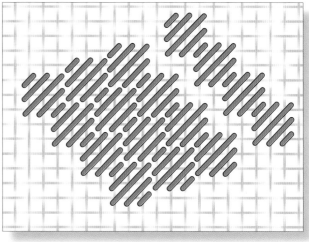

SHELL

This decorative stitch is worked in several stages. First the vertical bars are put in across six horizontal threads of canvas. Each stitch has five of these bars. The last in each group and the first of the next group share the holes of the canvas. Work these across the row.

Next, tie each group together with a horizontal stitch over the two central threads of canvas. You will need to angle the needle out from the stitches and tuck it back round each group.

Now the groups are linked together with one continuous surface thread. Starting somewhere to the left of the groups, thread the needle under the first holding stitch from top to bottom. Take the needle across to the second group and thread it through this group from bottom to top. Again take it through the first and second holding stitches in the same directions. Do not pull the yarn too tight.

Take the needle across to the third holding stitch and through from top to bottom, then back to the second holding stitch and through from bottom to top and finally to the third holding stitch and through from top to bottom. Continue across the row linking the groups, then work as many rows of the stitch as required.

To cover up any bare canvas that might show when finished, work a back stitch across two threads of canvas between each row where they meet.

Uses

This is a large, very decorative stitch with surface decoration.

Variations

The stitch can be worked without the looped thread, although this will leave canvas showing that will need to be covered with something else.

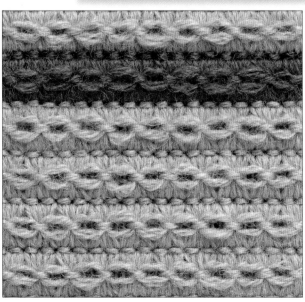

TENT

This is the simplest and most common stitch in canvaswork and the foundation for many other stitches. Tent stitch is usually worked across a single intersection of canvas from bottom left to top right. How you travel between tent stitches can be worked in several different ways, each with its own name: continental, basketweave and half cross.

Continental

This variant is worked in horizontal or vertical rows and makes a diagonal stitch on the back, larger than that on the front. This is a fairly hardwearing stitch.

Working from right to left, make a tent stitch from bottom left to top right. On the reverse of the canvas make a diagonal stitch across two threads of the canvas and bring the needle up one thread to the left of the bottom corner of the first canvas stitch. Continue across the row in the same way, making the stitches from bottom left to top right.

The back of this work will be dense rows of diagonal stitches, longer than those on the front.

To work a row from left to right, the order of the stitch is reversed: i.e. top right to bottom left.

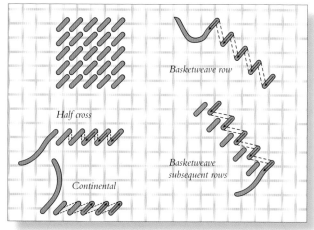

Basketweave row

Half cross

Basketweave subsequent rows

Continental

Basketweave

This is the most hardwearing of the three variants and the least likely to warp the canvas. It should always be used in large areas of tent stitch. It is worked in diagonal rows, either from the top right-hand corner down, or from the bottom left-hand corner up.

Working the tent stitch area from the bottom left-hand corner, make a diagonal row of tent stitches, each from top right to bottom left, and with a vertical stitch across two threads on the reverse. On the return row, fit the tent stitches

between those of the first row, this time making a horizontal stitch across two canvas threads on the reverse.

When working down a basketweave row, there will be a horizontal stitch on the reverse, and when working up a row there will be a vertical stitch on the reverse. When worked carefully the back of the work should have a neat woven appearance.

Half cross

This variant is worked in horizontal or vertical rows and uses the least amount of thread. It is also the least hardwearing variant and can warp the canvas if worked over a large area.

Working from right to left, make a tent stitch from top right to bottom left. On the reverse of the canvas make a vertical stitch down across one thread of canvas. Begin the next tent stitch, again working from top right to bottom left. The back of an area worked in half cross will be quite open and will all be vertical stitches.

To work a row from left to right, the order of the stitch is reversed: i.e. bottom left to top right.

Uses

Tent stitch is versatile and can be fitted into any shape. It is very useful for fitting into gaps left at the edges of other stitches.

Variations

The angle of this stitch can be reversed to lean from bottom right to top left. Rows of reversed tent stitch can be alternated with rows of tent stitch.

Related stitches

When worked on a single thread of double canvas this stitch is called petit point. It is often used for the small detailed areas of a design and combined with other stitches on double canvas.

Landscape

This landscape uses larger textural stitches in the foreground, which reduce in scale and texture to the horizon. Stranded cotton was used for the smoothly-blended sky. 21st century. (Personal collection of Yukari Suai)

Canvas chair seat

A canvas design by Nikki Jarvis,
worked by the RSN Studio staff
and apprentices. 20th Century.
(RSN Collection)

TURKEY RUG KNOT

This can be a looped or cut stitch depending on the desired effect. In both cases, it must be worked from the bottom upwards. With no knot and a loose tail end on the top of your canvas, take the needle down through the canvas where you wish to start. Bring the needle up one thread to the left of this. Holding the working loop of the thread to the top of the work, take the needle down two threads across from where it came up but do not pull it tight yet. Bring the needle back up where you initially started and pull the loop tight. This will form a horizontal holding stitch to the tail ends of the thread.

Take the needle to the right of the horizontal holding stitch and, again, without pulling the thread tight, loop it around to one canvas thread across from the last stitch. Take the needle down and bring it up one thread to the left of this, through the same hole as the previous stitch. Holding the working loop of the thread to the top of the work, take the needle down two threads across from where it came up but do not pull it tight yet. Bring the needle back up where it first began and pull the loop tight.

Continue looping stitches across the row. Cut the thread at the end of the row and return to the left-hand side of the work. Make a second row above the first, beginning one thread to the left, so that the stitches are bricked. When the area is complete the loops can either be left as they are (see the left-hand side of the photograph) or cut short for a more fluffy appearance (right-hand side of the photograph).

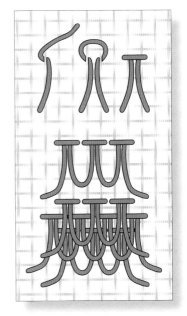

Uses

This stitch gives a very fluffy texture to an area and can give real height to the work. However, it is also very slow to work.

Turkey rug stitch should always be the last stitch to be put in your design as it is very difficult to fit other stitches around it due to its dense nature.

Related stitches

This stitch is also known as Ghiordes knot.

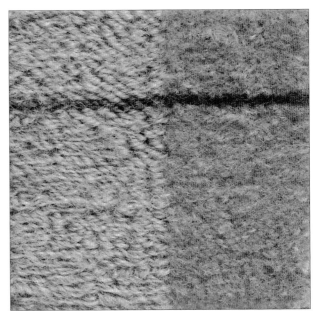

UPRIGHT CROSS

This is a small cross stitch worked upright. First make a vertical stitch across two canvas threads, then cross it with a horizontal stitch across two canvas threads. Make sure the top stitch is always horizontal. Work the crosses in horizontal rows. The second row should fit into the spaces of the first.

Uses

This is a very small stitch with a raised texture. It is particularly good for small areas.

Related stitches

This stitch is also known as straight cross stitch. This stitch can be alternated with a regular cross stitch across two by two canvas threads and it becomes reversed cross.

Bargello brooch

A Bargello pattern, cut out and applied to a brooch. 21st century. (Personal collection of Margaret Dier)

Dragon

A design influenced by a dragon on a William De Morgan ceramic vase. Large patterns are used individually in 'spots' on the background. 21st Century. (Personal collection of Jacqui McDonald)

VICTORIAN STEP

This is a diagonal stepped stitch worked in vertical stitches. Begin with a vertical stitch across four canvas threads. To the bottom right of this stitch make three vertical stitches across two canvas threads. In line with the top of these stitches, begin another long stitch over four canvas threads which should end two canvas threads below the last stitches.

Continue stepping the stitches, making three smaller stitches then one long one.

The second row should be fitted into the gaps of the first, with the first long stitch of the next row sitting to the left of the leftmost long stitch of the previous row. The top of the long stitch should be at the same level as the short stitches in the previous row.

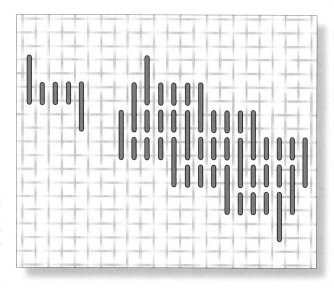

Uses

This stitch has a medium-sized pattern repeat and gives a smooth appearance of diagonal lines running through the area.

Variations

The steps can be made longer or shorter by increasing or decreasing the number of smaller stitches in each step.

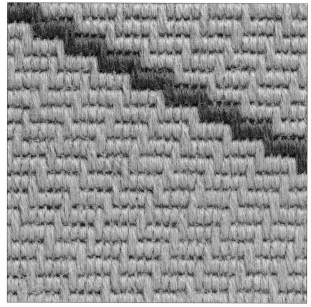

WEB

This stitch of couched diagonal lines gives a woven appearance. Begin at the top left-hand corner of the area with a cross stitch over two by two canvas threads. Make sure the top stitch goes from top left to bottom right. Start the next long stitch two threads down from the bottom left-hand corner of the cross stitch, and take it across to two threads to the right of the top of the cross stitch. Work back across this thread with diagonal stitches, always taking them from bottom right to top left and tucking them under the previous couched thread. Lay the next long thread and again couch back across it. Continue the pattern by laying threads and then immediately couching them down.

Uses

This stitch gives an even woven appearance without having to weave the threads.

Related stitches

If this stitch is worked horizontally, it becomes Bokhara couching.

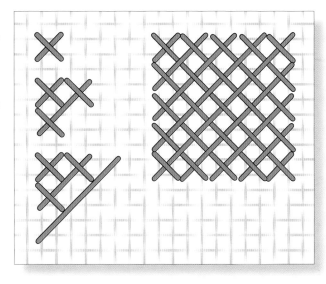

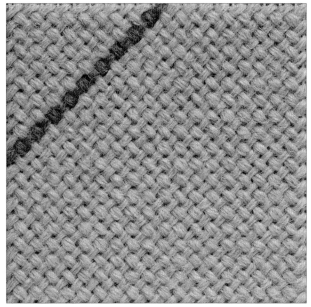

Moving on

STITCH BLENDING

Within an area of a design, several different stitches can be blended organically from one to the next, in order to create depth or texture or simply to create interest. Stitch blending needs to be gradual and with room to take place. One stitch stopping dead and another immediately starting will look too sudden. The second stitch needs to be introduced slowly into the pattern of the first.

The most successful blending of stitches occurs between stitches that are of a similar scale or direction: two diagonal stitches of similar sizes would be easy to blend, for example, while a large diagonal stitch would be difficult to blend into a small horizontal stitch.

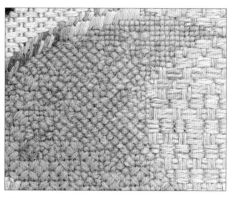

Here, from the bottom left corner upwards, the rice stitch is reduced in scale, and gradually becomes upright cross stitch. This is reduced again and becomes a simple cross stitch.

Magpies
21st century. (Author's personal collection)

Broad cross stitch is blended into a rice stitch by gradually introducing individual rice stitches into the broad cross pattern.

COLOUR BLENDING

Colour blending is an important part of any design. It will give shape to objects and depth to the design. Use your original image as a guide and refer to it constantly while stitching.

It is important to remember that you are stitching an interpretation of the original design. Due to the restrictions of the stitches and materials you are working with, you will not be able to get every detail into your piece. But that is part of the process. Choose what is important and leave out what is not.

Smooth shading

This is a controlled method of shading. The sky is worked in stranded cotton with a range of three shades to create the shaded effect. To blend smoothly from one shade to the next, the darkest shade was gradually faded out and the next shade gradually introduced across each diagonal line of the pattern. Work with several needles at once, each threaded up with a different shade. Do not try to change colour too quickly and try to be as free as possible with your shade placement.

Random shading

The field in the foreground is shaded in a more random way. This method uses blending in the needle. Three shades of crewel wool were used to create the effect. The shades were paired up into three different combinations, i.e. light with dark, light with medium and dark with medium. These were then all used at once in a completely random order to create a mottled effect.

Windmill

21st century. (Author's personal collection)

INDEX

A Piece of Cake

A group of cakes with surface stitched details and applied elements. The strawberry is a tent stitched slip, cut out and applied. 21st century. (Personal collection of Sophie Long)